11677721

D0706705

Economics
without
Equilibrium

THE ARTHUR M. OKUN MEMORIAL LECTURES
Yale University

Economics without Equilibrium

NICHOLAS KALDOR

With a Preface by James Tobin

M.E. SHARPE, INC.
Armonk, New York

Library of Congress Cataloging in Publication Data

Kaldor, Nicholas, 1908-
    Economics without equilibrium.

    ''The Okun memorial lectures at Yale University.''
    1. Economics—Addresses, essays, lectures. 2. Equilibrium (Economics)—Addresses, essays, lectures. I. Title.
HB71.K273   1985   339.5   85-1875
ISBN 0-87332-336-X

HB
71
K273
1985

Design by Angela Foote

Contents

Preface

By James Tobin

Nicholas Lord Kaldor delivered these three lectures at Yale University in October 1983, the first of a series in memory of Arthur M. Okun, who died suddenly, tragically prematurely, on March 23, 1980, at the age of 51.

The Arthur M. Okun Memorial Lectures have been made possible by gifts to Yale by an alumnus who was a long-time friend and admirer of Okun. The donor has stated the reasons for the series in these words:

> Arthur Okun combined his special gifts as an analytical and theoretical economist with his great concern for the well-being of his fellow citizens into a thoughtful, pragmatic, and sustaining contribution to his nation's public policy.
>
> Extraordinarily modest personally, he was a delightful and trenchant activist on behalf of others—both as members of our whole society and as individuals. He touched many, many people in ways they will always cherish.
>
> Offered in affectionate appreciation of Art's gifts, this lecture series seeks to recognize and encourage professional economists to search for policies that will contribute to the betterment of life and living.

Art Okun was a member of the Yale economics faculty from 1951 to 1969, although from the fall of 1961 he was mostly on leave for public service in Washington. When he came to Yale, he was completing his Ph.D. dissertation from Columbia, where he received his B.A. in 1949 and Ph.D. in 1956. He quickly became a bulwark of the Yale economics department, an intellectual and institutional leader.

Art was a marvelous and generous teacher and colleague. His office—door always open—was the place to go to get things straight, confusions dispelled, errors corrected, questions sensibly posed, models repaired. A thinker of natural integrity and inexhaustible curiosity, he pursued matters in depth, unsatisfied until logic was tight and facts fell into place. Patient and considerate in classroom and out, he could always find and foster some kernel of merit in even the most unpromising questions or comments.

In 1961 Art Okun joined the staff of President Kennedy's Council of Economic Advisers and began a brilliant career of public service. He returned to academia in fall 1963, but a year later President Johnson appointed him a Member of the Council, of which he became Chairman in 1968. When administrations changed in 1969, Okun resigned his Yale professorship and joined the Brookings Institution in Washington as a Senior Fellow.

At Brookings much of his energy and leadership went into his brainchild, the Brookings Panel on Economic Activity, which enlisted able theorists and econometricians from Brookings and elsewhere for research on the major macroeconomic events and policy issues of the day. The papers were published in *Brookings Papers on Economic Activity*, which under the painstaking editorship of Okun and George Perry became one of the most admired professional journals in economics. Art had organized a special meeting of the Panel and a special issue of *BPEA* for their tenth anniversary in 1980, but he did not live to take part.

Arthur Okun was a great economist, unerring in his intuition and his perception of the core of a problem or the essence of an argument. His unique chemistry compounded theory, insight, and hard-won fact into miracles of revelation. His expositions, even of difficult material, were models of clarity, grace, humor, and style. In the architecture and practice of economic policy he was simultaneously innovative and prudent. Both as scholar and policy-maker he was not only a realist but a humanist, unwavering in his conviction that economics and its applications could and should improve the welfare of actual human beings, mainly those who start the competitive race far behind.

No one could have been more fitting for the first lectures of the series than Lord Kaldor, one of the truly great economists of the world in this century. The committee charged with responsibility for the series, and the faculty and students of economics and other disciplines, were delighted that Lord Kaldor honored Yale and the memory of Arthur Okun by accepting our invitation.

Throughout a long and productive career Lord Kaldor has combined original and insightful innovations in economic theory, imaginative and pragmatic policy proposals, and distinguished public service. Like Okun, Kaldor has always sought to harness the art and science of economics to the betterment of the human condition. His bases have been London and the older Cambridge, but his interests and influence have covered the world. Like Okun, Kaldor has always been a free spirit and an independent mind, resisting classification in any "school" or ideology.

The reader will see that Lord Kaldor made a special point of relating his own views of economic process to those of Okun, particularly the theory of markets set forth in Okun's *magnum opus*, *Prices and Quantities*, posthumously published. Both Kaldor and Okun regard the standard price-cleared auction market model of the economy as unrealistic and therefore seriously misleading in its macroeconomic implications. Kaldor's lectures are a cogent critique of the standard model and an outline of the elements of a more relevant model, which can provide a solid microeconomic foundation for Keynesian macroeconomics.

Lord Kaldor's lectures drew a large, attentive, and enthusiastic audience at Yale. They deserve a much wider audience. We at Yale are proud to have the lectures in print, and we are grateful to M. E. Sharpe, Inc. for publishing them.

James Tobin
Sterling Professor of Economics
Yale University

New Haven
January 1985

I

Stylized Facts
as a Basis
for Theory Building

I feel both honored and pleased to have been asked to introduce the Okun Memorial Lectures which, I understand, are planned to become an annual feature of the courses given in this University. For many years I regarded Arthur Okun as one of the few economists—counting both sides of the Atlantic—whose interests and outlook were along the right lines, and who possessed the intellectual powers, the mental vigor, the gift of exposition, and the capacity for sustained exertion necessary for successfully advancing knowledge along these lines. I gained this view from his numerous writings scattered among many periodicals (though recently they appeared more frequently and prominantly in the *Brookings Papers on Economic Activity* of which he was a co-editor); from his posthumously published book *Prices and Quantities* (which presents a more thorough and systematic exposition of his ideas); and to a limited extent from personal acquaintance which was confined to occasional brief visits to the Brookings Institution in Washington and to occasional meetings at conferences. But whether I was listening to a speech of his at a conference or just engaged in lunchtime conversation, I invariably felt that I was in the presence of a man with an exceptional mind.

First, let me explain what I mean when I say that Arthur Okun was one of the few economists of his generation whose interests and outlook were along the right lines. His main motive was not the pursuit of economic theory for its own sake—the construction of more advanced theoretical models—but the severely practical motive of discovering methods or policies to improve the performance of the economy in terms of the twin objectives of efficiency and equality, that is, how to minimize the cost in terms of economic inequality of policies aiming at higher productivity or efficiency.

These are broadly the same objectives I myself, together with many of my colleagues, regard as making the study of economics worthwhile. But I particularly valued in Okun what I once called the method of proceeding by collecting "stylized facts" and then constructing a hypothesis that fits them. In other words, contrary to the prevailing trend, one should subordinate deduction to induction, and discover the empirical regularities first,whether through a study of statistics or through special inquiries that include "informal conversations with the owners or executives of small businesses" (and I presume, the executives of large businesses as well). One should also seek the most reasonable explanation capable of accounting for these "facts," independently of whether they fit into the general framework of received theory or not.

I called them "stylized facts," a term used also by Okun, because in the social sciences, unlike the natural sciences, it is impossible to establish facts that are precise and at the same time suggestive and intriguing in their implications, and that admit to no exception. So when we say, for example, that in the course of economic growth the profit rate or the capital/output ratio tends to remain constant, or that productivity varies procyclically whereas the variation in real wages is neither procyclical nor anticyclical, we do not imply that any of these "facts" are invariably true in every conceivable instance but that they are true in the broad majority of observed cases—in a sufficient number of cases to call for an explanation that would account for them. Such hypotheses relate to particular *aspects* of the economy and they may be suggestive of others. They may be discarded if they prove inconsistent with other observed features and then be replaced by something else.

In comparison with the high-sounding principles of the great systematizers, this kind of inductive-deductive theorizing may appear pedestrian. But it is far more likely to lead to a better understanding of how capitalist economies work than the all-embracing principles of the great system-builders who, in the field of economics at any rate, are more likely to obstruct the progress of knowledge than to promote it.

This contrast between the two types of cognition—the one derived from intuition and developed by means of *a priori* reasoning, and the other derived from observation, the discovery of empirical regularities or associations that yield hypotheses that can be refuted—is not peculiar of course to the social sciences. It has been just as prominent in the natural sciences with the difference, however, that for the last few centuries at least, nobody put forward a "general theory" based on deductive reasoning alone that could not be verified (or refuted) by observation if not by experiment. Einstein's theory of relativity was perhaps the last of the "grand ideas" derived from intuition alone, and though he pointed to specific ways in which his hypothesis could be verified (or refuted) by reference to certain aberrations in the movement of distant stars that could not be explained on Newtonian principles, it took five years before his prediction was empirically verified. And I gather that he spent the rest of his life trying to find a comprehensive theory for inanimate matter that would unify gravitation and electro-magnetic theory, and failed. He had little contact (so I understand) with the people who fitted the tiny particles that came from the big machines with a theoretical framework and who, advancing bit by bit (according to some authorities in Cambridge, England) are now getting near to such a comprehensive theory, which Einstein sought in vain.

However, in earlier phases of history, general theories concerning the nature of matter or the nature of the universe were not of a kind that were capable of being verified; all that was required of them was that their conclusions should follow logically from their premises, and that they should be derived from a consistent set of axioms by means of deductions that are logically correct. This was true even in those rare instances such as the Pythagorean theorem where the original discovery was supposed to have been due to empirical observations (in architecture in this case) and which was later "proved" by means of a purely logical argument with the aid of geometry. Archimedes was one of the first scientists in the ancient world who resembled modern scientists in seeking a hypothesis for explaining specific phenomena that could be verified by experiment. His law concerning the weight of bodies immersed in water was precise and was capable of experimental confirmation. But taken by itself, it did not help in formulating general laws relating to the universe (though it proved fully consistent with such laws when they were formulated 1800 years later).

General economic theory, by this test, has not really progressed beyond the stage of the natural philosophy of the Greeks, though of course it makes use of enormously more sophisticated mathematical tools. It developed, with a high degree of sophistication, the logical (or mathematical) properties of economic equilibrium, the purpose of which is to explain how the price mechanism serves to coordinate the actions of millions of individual "agents" acting independently of each other, but without investigating at any stage whether its basic axioms correspond to reality or not, or whether the propositions derived from them by deductive methods can be verified. As Professor Roy Weintraub wrote (in the *Journal of Economic Literature* of March 1983) at the end of a recent survey of the development of the theory of competitive equilibrium, "the 'equilibrium' story is one in which empirical work, ideas of facts and falsification, played no role at all."

Whether such a claim is true or not, it is clear that the axioms of the general equilibrium theory of Walras (as amended by Wald, Arrow, Debreu, McKenzie, and others) contain assertions about the real world that can be refuted and without which the main conclusions of the theory would *not* hold, as for example, those relating to the laws of production. There are other axioms that are demonstrably untrue; for example, that all prices are given parametrically to all "agents" and prices constitute the sole kind of information on which decisions are based or that the economy operates without either material or monetary inventories or reserves. And finally there are axioms that, though non-tautological, are incapable, in practice, of being verified or refuted; for example, that the action of all agents is guided solely by the criterion of "optimization" by which is meant that producers maximize their profits or consumers their "utility."

Outline of These Lectures

At this stage I will give the plan of these lectures to make it easier to follow what I shall be driving at. The first lecture—or rather the remainder of this lecture—will deal with the question of how markets work and why their manner of functioning precludes a pure price system of market clearing, and what is the role of quantity signals as distinct from price signals.

The second lecture deals with the question of how prices are formed and how competition operates in the quasi-competitive or quasi-monopolistic markets that embrace a very large part of a modern industrial economy, and it points up the large and important areas of ignorance, where more knowledge could be gained by well directed research.

The third lecture gives an outline of an alternative approach, which looks upon the economy as a continually evolving system whose path cannot be predicted any more than the evolution of an ecological system in biology. I shall attempt to outline the implications in terms of "cumulative causation"—or virtuous and vicious circles—which is excluded from the world of traditional economics.

Returning to prevailing theory, as far as I understand it, the axioms of equilibrium theory were originally chosen in order to secure the desired result, in other words, the assumptions required for proving the existence of a unique and possibly stable general equilibrium.* But its authors were motivated by the belief that they were only laying the foundations of an explanation of how a market economy works, an initial stage of the analysis which is in the nature of "scaffolding": it has to be erected before the permanent building can be built, but will be removed step by step as the permanent building nears completion. However, since Walras first wrote down his system of equations over 100 years ago, progress has definitely been backwards not forwards in the sense that the present set of axioms are far more restrictive than those of the original Walrasian model. The ship is no nearer to the shore, but considerably farther off, though in a logical, mathematical sense, the present system of derived tautologies is enormously superior to Walras's original effort.

Perhaps for that reason general equilibrium theory retains its fascination for teachers and students of economics alike. Indeed, judging by the number of Ph.D. students working on the implications of the rational expectation hypothesis, it is gaining ground, at any rate, in America. One reason is the intuitive belief that the price mechanism is the key to everything, the key instrument in guiding the operation of an undirected, unplanned, free market economy. The Walrasian model and its most up-to-date successor may both be highly artificial abstractions from the real world but the truth

*Specifically, a state of equilibrium is defined as one in which at the ruling system of prices, the supplies and demands of all commodities are equal (no unsatisfied buyers or sellers) and no improvement in anyone's position is possible without a worsening of someone else's position.

that the theory conveys—that prices provide the guide to all economic action—must be fundamentally true, and its main implication that free markets secure the best results must also be true. (This second propositon was indeed demonstrated but under assumptions so restrictive that Professor Hahn turned the argument around and suggested, in his inaugural lecture, that the importance of general equilibrium theory lies precisely in showing how stringent the conditions must be for "free markets" to secure the results in terms of welfare that are naively attributed to them. This may well be true, but if so, it is truth bought at a very high cost.)

But the basic assumption in all this—that prices are very important in the working of a market economy—is rarely, if ever, questioned. Yet it is precisely this overemphasis on the role of the price system that I regard as the major shortcoming of modern neoclassical economics, particularly the Walrasian version of it.

The Role of Dealers and Speculators

Walras knows only two categories of "agents": producers and consumers. He makes no mention of the third category which is vital to the functioning of any market economy, namely, the "dealer" or "middleman" (or "merchant") who is neither buyer nor seller, because he is both simultaneously. It is the dealers or merchants who make a "market" which enables producers to sell and consumers to buy, and who carry stocks of the commodity they deal in in large enough amounts to tide over any discrepancies between outside sellers and outside buyers over any short period of time, and in practice fulfill the role designed for the "heavenly auctioneer" since they are the people who at any moment of time quote prices for purchases or for sales. They are not required under actual rules to buy or sell only at "equilibrium" prices—whatever that is taken to mean—though there are special markets, like the London bullion market, where the actual dealing price is struck after ascertaining the demands and the offers of dealers at various prices. (This is possible when, as in the London gold market, everybody's demand and supply can be handled through a small number of dealers.) At any given moment of time, or to be a little more realistic, at the start of business, say, the first thing in the morning, all prices are given to them as a heritage of the past. The important thing is that it is the dealers who initiate the price changes necessary for aligning, or rather realigning, the demand of the consumers and the supply of producers. They make their living on the "turn" between the buying price and the selling price; and the larger the market and the greater the competition between dealers, the less this "turn" is likely to be, as a proportion of price (always provided that the "turn" must be large enough to cover interest and carrying costs on stocks plus some compensation for the risk of a fall in market prices in the future). Thus buying or selling necessarily involves transaction costs that cannot be said to fall on the seller any more than on the buyer; they are divided between them, but it is not meaningful to ask how much falls on one side rather than the other.

Any discrepancy between sales and purchases (of "outsiders," that is, of producers and consumers) is simultaneously reflected in the stocks (or "inventories" to use the American term) carried by merchants. Experience has taught them how large their "normal" stocks need to be in relation to their turnover in order to ensure continuity of dealing, for a dealer's reputation (or good will) depends on his ability to satisfy his customers at all times; refusal or inability to deal is likely to divert business to others. They protect their stock by varying *both* their buying and selling prices simultaneously, raising prices when stocks are falling and lowering them when they are rising.

The size of price variation induced by a change in the volume of stocks held by the market depends on the dealer's expectations of how long it will take before prices return to "normal," and how firmly such expectations are held. Even before the Second World War, the short-term fluctuations in commodity market prices (i.e., the markets of the staple agricultural and industrial raw materials, including metals) were very large. According to Keynes's calculations in 1938 (in an article in the *Economic Journal*)* the *average annual variation* in the ten previous years between the lowest and the highest prices in the *same* year in the case of four commodities (rubber, cotton, wheat, and lead) was 67 percent. Unfortunately, the corresponding figures for the fluctuations in stocks carried that were associated with these price variations were not stated, but it is pretty obvious that such price variations could not have taken place unless there were frequent changes in the prevailing expectations concerning future supplies or demands.

Nor is it known how far the price movements were exaggerated as a result of the activities of yet another class of "agents," the speculators. Professional dealers act under the influence of price expectations, and to

---

*"The Policy of Government Storage of Food Stuffs and Raw Materials." *Economic Journal*, September 1938, pp. 449–460.

that extent their market behavior can also be regarded as speculative in character. But their actions are motivated by the desire to *reduce* the risks facing them (which they inevitably assume as dealers) by their willingness to reduce their stocks in times of high prices and the opposite willingness to absorb extra stocks when prices are regarded as abnormally low. In any case the risks they carry are an inevitable by-product of their function as dealers. Speculators on the other hand *assume* risks for the sake of a gain and thereby provide facilities for hedging by buying "futures" from those who are committed to carry stocks of a commodity, and selling "futures" to those who are committed (by their productive activities) to acquire commodities in the future for uses for which they have already entered contractual commitments.

The activities of both dealers and speculators are supposed to smooth out both fluctuations in prices and variations in the size of inventories. Price rises should be moderated by the reduction of inventories held by dealers; similarly, a price fall should be moderated by a consequential increase in inventories. As Arthur Okun pointed out in one of his last papers,* as a matter of "stylized fact" this is the very opposite of what actually happens.

> The hallmark of U.S. postwar recessions has been inventory liquidation, following a major buildup of inventories at the peak of the expansion. Standard models that assume price-taking and continuous market clearing do not suggest that a

*Rational Expectations with Misperceptions As a Theory of the Business Cycle, proceedings of a seminar held in February 1980 and printed in the *Journal of Money, Credit and Banking*, November 1980, Part 2.

disappointment about relative prices will lead traders to liquidate inventories. For example, a sudden
drop in the demand for, and hence the price of wheat
that leads farmers to decrease production in the
future will generally lead traders to increase stocks
initially. (The price tends to fall enough currently
relative to its new future expected value to provide
traders with that incentive.) Why then, in the business cycle, is an aggregate cut back in production
accompanied by a cutback in stocks?

This was mentioned as the first of eight "stylized cyclical facts" that Okun regarded as inconsistent with the
rational expectations hypothesis; it related to the behavior of a special class of "agents" whose main business it is to be rational in their expectations.

All this related mainly to the behavior of commodity
markets which come nearer to the "auction markets"
of general equilibrium theory than all the other "markets" in the economy. Yet they fail to satisfy the theoretical requirements from more than one point of view.
First, they are not "market clearing" in the sense of
equating demand and supply on the strict criterion that
the maximum amount sellers desire to sell at the ruling
price is equal to the maximum buyers desire to buy.
There is a change in inventories from period to period,
held by *insiders* in the market, that is quite un-Walra-
sian—it means that demand was either in excess of, or
short of, supply—the market has not "cleared," and the
transactions, even in the shortest of periods, such as a
day or even an hour, did not take place at a uniform
price but at prices that varied sometimes minute by
minute.

The Role of Business Goodwill

Secondly, even in the most highly organized markets, business dealings are far from anonymous. Though the prices offered or demanded by the various dealers tend to be the same, at any one point of time for exactly the same variant in terms of quality, delivery dates, and so on, it is part of human nature for buyers to have customary suppliers. That does not mean one supplier, but generally a limited circle of dealers each of whom will receive a fairly steady share of a particular buyer's custom. As R. G. Hawtrey put it in a highly stimulating book that is rarely read nowadays, "Everyone concerned will tend, in the absence of any reason to the contrary, to follow his established routine, and to deal in the *way* he knows with the *people* he knows. This continuity in dealings creates what is called business connexion or goodwill. It is the very stuff and substance of the dealer's business."*

The basic reason is that a decision to buy is influenced, even in the simplest of cases, by a complex set of information (other than that relating to price) for which the buyer is mainly dependent on the knowledge, acumen, honesty, and reliability of the dealer. There is a wool market, for example, although there is not just one kind of wool, but hundreds of kinds; the same is true of cotton, jute, wheat, or sugar. General equilibrium theory would say all this is elementary; each of these variants has a special product number, and this relates not only to the many aspects of quality but to differences in availability in time and space.

*R. G. Hawtrey, *The Economic Problem*, London 1926, p. 39.

The point is that they are part of a single market, intermediated by the same set of dealers, and their price movements are generally, though not invariably, subject to the same influences. There is a wool market and a cotton market, and there is a market for cargo—for shipping space. A theoretical approach that ignores the way markets are organized in the real world for the sake of logical or mathematical purity is not likely to come up with conclusions that will improve our understanding of how things work. (Hawtrey's contention that everyone likes to deal "with the people they know and who know their ways" is true even in the market for financial assets, such as the Stock Exchange, where people prefer to deal with their accustomed broker, though each different "product" is clearly numbered and labeled and one particular bond is just as good as any other of the same issue and confers exactly the same rights.)

Objection may of course be raised that in the *pure* Walrasian model there is one market for all the m products or all the n(m) products, that is, m products for each of n periods, or all the n(m)(s) products, meaning n(m) products in s points in space; and what Walras, with the help of Wald, Debreu, Arrow, and others, has demonstrated is that there exists a single system of prices relating to all these products capable of clearing all n(m)(s) markets at the same moment of time, assuming that nothing takes time—all production plans, production, selling intention and actual sale, planned and actual purchases and their consumption occur at the same moment. In other words, problems of time are eliminated by collapsing time as a dimension and afterwards drawing it out again so that each successive moment or unit of time is an exact replica of the previous moment (or unit). Even then it is not clear what happens at any moment subsequent to the first, since in some versions of general equilibrium theory *all* transactions for *all* future periods are made simultaneously at the beginning.

Again, this is not of course what Walras meant or intended—any superficial glance at his book makes it evident that this is not so. For example, he presupposes a demand for desired cash balances because "agents" are paid on Fridays and spend their money on Tuesdays (or something like it), which incidentally does not quite fit the "Walrasian Law." But they are the assumptions necessary as shown by later writers, to make the concept of a unique equilibrium set of prices embracing all products logically or mathematically watertight.

The question is, does the "paradigm" reveal something important about the forces that guide capitalist market economies? This amounts to the same as saying: can the manifestly absurd or unreal assumptions of equilibrium theory be abandoned while still preserving the "core" of the theory—which I take to be the proposition that the movement of relative prices of commodities and labor enables us to have enough fresh bread baked every morning, that people enter the professions in such relative numbers as are necessary to ensure that there is no penury of dentists nor a plethora of doctors or a superfluity of lawyers, and the same is true of street cleaners, sewage workers, motor car mechanics, and so on.

Price Fluctuations in Commodity Markets

The big commodity markets in "staples" are undoubtedly the nearest real-world equivalent of the purely competitive and wholly price-flexible auction markets of the textbooks. Yet in some ways they are the least satisfactory feature of capitalist market economies, as is shown by the extent and frequency of government intervention regarding prices and also in the regulation of supplies. In the absence of these they exhibit the largest instabilities in prices, with price fluctuations regularly going up and down like a yo-yo even when the variations in the rate of production and consumption around the trend are rather small. Moreover, as Professor Sylos Labini has shown recently,* the range of fluctuations in commodity prices in response to changes in the growth rate of world industrial production (which governs the demand for them) has been nearly three times as great in the post-1971 period as it was before. The only rational explanation I can offer of why commodity markets performed so much worse since 1971 is that, despite the postwar inflationary trend up to the early 1970s, the belief in a long-run "normal price" of commodities, in terms of gold or dollars, lingered on, and was only shocked out of existence by President Nixon's somewhat symbolic suspension of the gold convertibility of the dollar (I say "somewhat symbolic" since *de facto* convertibility was already restricted by earlier measures) on August 15, 1971. Belief in a long-run normal price of a commodity has always been regarded as an indispensable condition for the reasonable functioning of commodity markets, since this ensures that any price movement upwards or downwards, however well supported by the nature of current events and the enthusiasm of outside speculators, is reversed at a certain point when the insiders come to feel that the price has moved too far

*See the graph and references in my paper in *Lloyds Bank Review*, July 1983.

from the long-run norm. The stronger the belief in the normal price, the nearer are the points of turn-round in price fluctuation.

However, the sudden sharp reversal of price movements since 1971 could have had little to do with the old idea of prices sooner or later reverting to some normal level, and had more to do with the conviction that leading governments were bound to counteract by monetary and fiscal policies both inflationary trends and economic recessions when they proceeded too far. But these judgments, based on the expectation of political measures acting on demand, provide much less of a "point of anchorage" for future prices than the old expectations based on supply adjustments occurring whenever the price deviated from long-run normal costs of production.

The Role of Quantity Signals

I have spent considerable time on the commodity markets because they represent the only sector of the economy where both the outside sellers and the outside buyers are "price-takers" and therefore where direct quantity signals—meaning a direct adjustment of production to changes in demand—can be ruled out, and adjustments of production can take place only in response to price incentives. But in all other fields, at least in the present century, the sellers, whether manufacturers or distributors, are price-*makers* and not price-*takers*, and changes in supply are the result of quantity signals rather than price signals. Quantity signals can be one of two kinds, or a combination of them: a change in the amount of stock carried or a change in the size of the producer's order book.

Stocks (or inventories) are carried by all those producers who make standard-type articles, where the buyer (whether an ultimate buyer, or an intermediary, a wholesale or a retail merchant) is accustomed to obtaining delivery within a short period, which is only possible by getting the particular article "off the shelf" of the manufacturer. Order books mainly relate to custom-built articles, whether ships, specially designed houses, or suits made by bespoke tailors, and where the buyer is expected to wait much longer for delivery after giving his orders, but if possible not too long, so that manufacturers of these latter categories of goods carry input stocks to save time and possible uncertainty of obtaining the inputs necessary for fabrication. Even the manufacturer of standard articles is likely to sell numerous varieties of the same commodity (think of shoes, cameras, detective novels, motor cars, refrigerators, and cookers) all of which make use of much the same materials but are of a somewhat different design, requiring only small differences in fabrication (e.g., when an otherwise identical car is painted red or blue). In all these cases the possession of a large input stock puts the manufacturer in a far more favorable position to satisfy his customers than possession of output stocks. He is likely to satisfy customers more easily and certainly more cheaply, since the ability to switch the use of an input from one variety to another can mean a large economy in stockholding as against the situation in which the manufacturer aims to keep a normal stock of all possible varieties of *finished* products.

The important conclusion is that the signal that causes an economic "agent" to do something different—produce more or produce less, or switch his manufacturing facilities from some varieties to others—is always a quantity signal, not a *price* signal. Prices are set by the producers on normal costs of production (or rather, on the costs calculated by reference to normal utilization of capacity) including a customary percentage added for profit; and within limits, the producer will not change his price as a result of a faster (or slower) increase in orders, unless the increase in demand signaled to him is so large that he cannot cope with it without disappointing his regular customers, or else the fall in demand is so large that it causes him to incur standstill costs due to lack of orders (keeping workers and machinery idle), in which case he might try to avoid some of these untoward consequences by some temporary price concession or a price concession that is not formally announced but that he is willing to concede in bargaining. In any case, in the actual adjustment of supply and demand, prices play only a very subordinate role, if any. If prices do change in the course of adjustment, these are incidental to the process of adjustment, and more likely to be a temporary rather than a permanent feature unless the commodity happens to be one in which increasing returns are important, in which case the increase in demand might indirectly lead to a reduction of prices.

Quantity signals are invariably prompt. The producer's stock is reduced simultaneously with the increase in his sales, and he has an incentive to raise production immediately so as to restore stocks to the normal level. He can decide later on whether the increase in his sales proves sufficiently large and lasting to call for an increase in his production capacity, either by hiring more workers, installing additional equipment, or both. Since the producer (or seller) sets the price, the large-scale advertising. It is from that period that the present age of monopolistic competition, accompanied by price and wage rigidity, can be said to have originated. And the change did far more than change the power relationship between wholesalers and manufacturers; it enabled the successful manufacturing firm to expand operations both by increasing its capacity ahead of demand and by diversifying production. It made it possible for successful firms to expand much faster than before, and therefore realize the economies of large-scale production more fully (as was the case with Ford); it was also the basis for the twentieth century development of the large multi-product corporations—the conglomerates.

II

Supply and Demand

he had had the chance to follow up his book with others. These questions will form the main theme of the second lecture. Some of them are not intended to provide definite answers, but rather to point up the areas of our ignorance. To an extent that is not often realized, or conceded, we do not really know how a modern capitalist market economy works, though given the right orientation for research, it should not prove too difficult to discover the answers.

The Stock-Adjustment Principle

The first and probably the most important conclusion (first stated, I believe, by Professor Kornai*) is that a wholly decentralized system, in which each firm makes its decisions regarding production and purchase quite independently, and reacts only to such signals as are observable *within* the factory gate, can operate based on information confined to its own sales and changes in its own input and output stock. It is only in regard to the flow of information that different firms are in contact. An order for a certain quantity of a commodity is a communication between two decision makers. This flow of information is linked to the physical flow of products. The information flow is also decentralized; buyer/seller pairs enter into informational contacts separately. Hence it follows that under certain assumptions (which we shall indicate in broad outline), a perfectly decentralized abstract system can operate without price signals, through the operation of the stock-adjustment principle. The main assumption is that each producing unit (each firm) is guided by the desire to maintain a certain normal output stock and

*The Economics of Shortage, North Holland, 1981.

a normal input stock. These norms are themselves related to the unit's sales and to its purchases, which in
turn are determined by its own production. When sales
increase stocks diminish; this leads to an increase in
output with a view of replacing stocks. If the increase
in sales is permanent, the increase in production will
also be permanent, accompanied by a larger temporary
increase until the desired relationship of stocks to sales
is regained. Kornai calls this the "vegetative control"
of economic processes, referring to the analogy of the
special role played by the vegetative nervous system
in the function of higher organisms. The role of stocks,
as was mentioned in my first lecture, could be replaced
by the role of order books; moreover there is nothing to
exclude both systems—stocks and order books—play-
ing a role side by side.

Demand-Constrained and
Resource-Constrained Economies

To say that production adjusts to quantity signals is
not to deny the importance of prices, since the quantity
signals themselves are influenced by relative prices,
particularly between goods that are close substitutes
to each other. The allocation of demand between broad
categories of expenditure (such as food, clothing, or
housing) is probably not greatly influenced by relative
prices, given the same income level. But within each of
these groups are subgroups, and subgroups within subgroups, and the narrower the group the more prices
are likely to influence the composition of quantity signals. It is through direct or indirect price-advantages
that new commodities manage to displace existing
ones.

This method of resource allocation presupposes that

production in general is demand-constrained and not resource-constrained. It cannot operate in a truly resource-constrained situation since the quantity signals cannot be made effective if there are no inputs available for the adjustment of production. In my first lecture I used the example of a market system turning out doctors, dentists, lawyers, etc. in the right relationships. Neoclassical theory asserts that it is the price system that operates so as to achieve this result. Applicants will flock to the professions where earnings are relatively high, and vice versa, and there is an equilibrium set of relative earnings that will achieve the right numerical relationships. There are a number of difficulties with this explanation, one of which is that differences *within* a group may swamp any differences *between* groups. Another is the existence of what Cairnes called "non-competing groups," which alone can explain why some of the most unpleasant jobs are often the worst paid, instead of the other way round. With the quantity signal principle, people are automatically "slotted in" more or less in proportion to the jobs available, with the next candidate filling the next vacancy. But this presupposes that there is always a queue of people waiting to get jobs (or preferably several queues for different types of labor—skilled, unskilled, highly trained, etc.).

In ensuring a demand-constrained economy, prices have a very important role to play, since the limitation of demand is only ensured by the budget constraint, and the very notion of a "budget constraint" presupposes that different commodities can be brought to a common measuring rod that enables the total purchasing power or buying power to be measured in value terms; it is the relation of the prices of goods to the level of incomes that determines the "budget constraint" of each participant in the market. (Professor Kornai has also introduced the distinction between "hard" and "soft" budget constraints, mainly relating to producers rather than consumers. In a capitalist economy the distinction applies to both.)

As we all know, it was Keynes's contention that a capitalist economy is normally demand-constrained, whereas the contention of the orthodox economists, whether the Walrasian general equilibrium school or other variants, is that under conditions of competition each resource will be fully employed: whatever unemployment there may be will be voluntary, not involuntary. Are we to take it that the battle between Keynes and the classicists was a sham battle in the sense that while Keynes was fundamentally right that the economy is demand-constrained and not resource-constrained, he was wrong in thinking that it could be anything else in a modern, non-Walrasian economy where prices do not and cannot fulfill a general market-clearing function.

The Role of Disguised Unemployment

The answer to this paradox, I believe, is that an economy does not cease to be demand-constrained merely because it attains "full employment" in some conventionally accepted sense of the term. The main reason for this is that mainly because of imperfect competition there is a large amount of "disguised unemployment" even in the most advanced countries, as shown by the fact that there is always a large queue of people in low-paid jobs who move to higher paid jobs as openings become available. As a result of this the normal response to an increased demand for labor, say in manufacturing, is that there is an automatic transference from low paid jobs in services (the loss of which moreover need not result in any measurable loss of output since it would be offset by the rise in productivity of those remaining in the labor-losing sectors). Imperfect competition has rather different effects in small-scale trades such as cafes, bars, restaurants, or retail shops than in the oligopolies. In small-scale trades the number of units existing at any one time is limited only by the existence of a break-even point. Hence their number tends to be such that there are a proportion of firms that operate at or above the minimum that enables them to cover costs, and not at the maximum set by their capacity. Since labor costs form a large proportion of total costs and labor in these trades is more in the nature of overhead costs, a loss of labor will be associated with an improvement in wages and a corresponding increase in minimum level of sales that cover costs, which means that the same total sales will be distributed among a smaller number of units. A reduction in open unemployment will therefore tend to be associated with a diminution in disguised unemployment that may be quantitatively just as large. (I cannot claim any expertise on the United States economy but it seems to me that one possible explanation of the break in the productivity trend after 1973 was the extraordinary increase in the number of jobs in the consumer service sectors—in restaurants, cafes, and so on—together with stagnant or falling employment in manufacturing.) The usual explanation for all this is that with the progress in real incomes per head, people want fewer goods and more services and that productivity growth in services is notoriously low. It is quite possible, however, that the big rise in employment in small-scale service enterprises was a *consequence* of a lower overall demand for labor, or a lower demand in the relatively high earning manufacturing industries. If that were the explanation it would show up in enlarged differences between earnings in manufacturing and earnings in services, something that could easily be investigated, if it hasn't been already. I am not suggesting of course that this could provide the *whole* explanation. A major part may be due to lower overall growth rates of demand (in real terms) which is associated with lower employment growth as well as lower productivity growth.

This is not to deny of course that the pressure of demand in an economy can become too large, and when this happens it shows itself in the appearance of bottlenecks at various points, increasing delays in delivery, and enforced slackness due to the unavailability of complementary goods. Britain in wartime and in the immediate postwar years exhibited these symptoms, but they appear to be chronic in socialist countries and the cause of a great deal of inefficiency of performance. Professor Kornai attributes this to the absence of effective budget constraints on business enterprises that cannot go bust or be liquidated even though they have continuing losses, as well as to an insatiable appetite for new investment, so that the number of projects started, or in train, generally exceeds the volume initially planned.

Inflation and Employment

In capitalist countries, in my own view, the change is the other way around: the constraints on the pressure of demand tend to be excessive, with the result that unemployment is much greater than can be justified by the needs of resource-allocation, and the rate of economic growth is appreciably less than it could be. The main reason for this is that the distribution of power and, ultimately, the distribution of incomes, changes in favor of labor the faster the economy grows and the nearer it is to full employment, and over a longer period it changes in favor of capital the greater the volume of unemployment. This is the real reason why the continuance of Keynesian policies after the war led to a recrudescence of long-discredited ideas that go by the name of "monetarism." The main attraction of monetarism was not its intellectual simplicity—inflation is a matter of the money supply, period—but that it elevated the fear of inflation to the unique position which could not be justified by the experience of numerous countries who habitually suffer from it. Thus the present British Government regards any kind of inflation as the greatest evil, and it managed to convince the public of the view that low unemployment is incompatible with the absence of inflation.

The most popular, and I would say almost universally accepted explanation for the link between inflation and employment is the Phillips Curve, an inverse correlation between unemployment and the rate of increase in money wages, which most economists intuitively feel to be true even though they admit that the relationship is not a stable one; some even describe it as a piece of statistics in search of a theory. In my own view the explanation lies elsewhere, even though it is consistent with the Phillips Curve as a piece of description, particularly of an unstable one. For reasons that are close to those held by Arthur Okun—the sense of "fairness" of business corporations that causes them to increase money wages even in circumstances where there is manifestly no compulsion on them to do so, an aspect of Okun's "invisible handshake"—there is a positive correlation between the rate of growth of profits and the rate of increase in money wages. Though profits fluctuate far more than wages, and the profit result of any single year may have little direct influence on the rise in wage payments, I believe I am right in saying that, taking a run of years, the rate of growth of profits is a very important influence on the rate of wage increases granted by the firm. There are several reasons for this, one of which is that successful firms like to pay higher wages than their competitors; this secures better labor relations and enables them to fill vacancies more promptly. The other reason is that where labor is unionized, firms are in a weak position to resist wage increases when wages form a declining proportion of the value of net output. On the other hand, given the method of mark-up pricing on direct costs (which, according to Okun, appears to be the predominant method in the United States), every increase in wages will raise profits, since for each unit of output, much the same percentage is added to value-added as is added to wages. As a result of this dual relationship—the discretionary wage increases which follow profit increases and the automatic profit increases caused by wage increases—a higher rate of output growth should cause not only a higher rate of inflation but accelerating inflation, though given the rate of growth, the acceleration will be at a decelerating rate and should ultimately settle down to some constant rate.

I am therefore in full agreement with Okun's view that incomes policy is indispensable if we wish to have a satisfactory and stable growth rate combined with reasonable stability in the value of money. Indeed my first memorandum on the subject to Stafford Cripps, the then Chancellor of the Exchequer, is dated June 1951, 34 years ago. I still think that the scheme I then put forward was an ingenious one. The only trouble with it, as a British Treasury official in charge of incomes policy pointed out to me a few years ago, is that it is still at least 25 years ahead of its time. For all kinds of political reasons, progress in this field is painfully slow, and as recent British and American experience testifies, it is sometimes negative.

The Mark-Up and the Share of Profits

We need to explain what determines the mark-up and why it is stable. I find no difficulty in explaining why the mark-up is generally calculated on *normal* capacity utilization (on standard volumes), for any attempt by a single producer to recoup the higher overheads (at low utilization of capacity) by increasing his price strongly tempts his competitors to achieve the same result by *not* following suit and thereby attaining the same end by gaining sales at his expense.

According to Okun, mark-up rigidity seems to be "simply too pervasive across the United States economy to be attributable to oligopoly."* Mark-up rigidity is not limited to automobiles, computers, and aluminum, but extends to nonconcentrated sectors like retail trades, an "industry which is as atomistic as any trustbuster could wish,"** as Okun said.

*Arthur M. Okun, *Prices and Quantities*, The Brookings Institution, 1981, pp. 175–176.
**Ibid., p. 176.

The question that needs examining more carefully is that of "mark-up rigidity." If it is based on an examination of the pricing behavior of individual firms in an industry, its implications are that either different firms charge very different prices or else the costs of different firms are identical or at least very similar.

There is one source of evidence that contradicts this, and I am frankly very surprised that more attention has not been paid to it, either by Arthur Okun, or, as far as I know, by anyone else in recent years.* This is the evidence on the very large differences in productivity (output per head) and on unit costs between different firms in the *same* industry. In Britain, recent evidence is very hard to come by on this matter, and my own views are based on figures published some considerable time ago. There are three different sources from which such figures can be derived: from statistics derived from income tax returns, from the periodic Censuses of Production which in the United Kingdom is collected every five years, and from a comparison of the figures disclosed in company accounts which are collated and analyzed mainly by specialized agencies (like Moodie's in England) for the purpose of investment advice.

In the United Kingdom the laws on the protection of business secrecy represent—rightly or wrongly—a strong obstacle to the disclosure of figures on the frequency distribution of productivity, costs, and profits. Thus for brief periods, both prewar and postwar, the Inland Revenue published fairly detailed figures regarding the percentage share of wages, material costs,

---

*The only book (to my knowledge) that tackled this question directly is Jack Downie's *The Competitive Process*, Duckworth, London, 1958.

rents, interest payments, depreciation, and net profit, not only for the average of each industry, but the frequency distribution ranked by the share of profit in sales. These figures appeared for some years in the 1920s, following evidence supplied to the *Colwyn Committee*, and were then suppressed on the insistence, I gather, of the then Chancellor of the Exchequer, Stanley Baldwin. They reappeared after the war under the Labor Government, only to be suppressed again on the return of the Tories; afterwards the figures were no longer collected. (Business organizations are extremely sensitive on this question for reasons that are not wholly clear to me.*)

The same secrecy surrounds the *individual* returns on which the Census of Production figures are based, and to my knowledge these were made available on one occasion only—in the early 1960s—to the then newly established National Economic Development Council and written up in an unpublished paper by R. G. Lipsey and F. G. Brechling. I am not familiar with United States studies on this, though I feel sure they must exist somewhere, and have a vague recollection of being told (some years ago) that they give much the same picture as the British figures.

The two British sources present much the same picture. According to the Census of Production material which is broken down by "establishments" (an establishment can comprise a number of factory buildings provided they have a common address), the value of net output (value added) per worker is four times as high in the highest tenth of establishments (weighted by

---

*The reasons why a "firm's costs of production are one of its most jealously guarded secrets" are analyzed by Downie, *op. cit.*, p. 89.

employment) than in the lowest tenth: while the differences in the share of profits are proportionate to this: the share of gross profit in value added varied (calculated as the difference between value added and labor costs) from 80 to 20 percent. (The difference in wages per worker, though positively correlated with output per worker, amounted to very little, and was only 10 percent.) These figures related to the average of 22 industry groups.

The Inland Revenue figures relate to firms, not establishments, and they show that at the top end the share of profit in value added amounted to more than 50 percent of value added for the top 10 percent and for only 15 percent at the bottom end, giving a ratio of value added per worker of 2:1 (it is to be expected that the differences between *firms* should be less than those between *establishments*).*

From what I have seen of the share of profits and employee costs in value added from stockbrokers' compilations of company accounts, they share much the same variation between the top end and the average, though naturally they have no interest in compiling figures at the bottom end.

Since firms do not willingly forego profits or cause losses, one must suppose they were under some compulsion by market forces. Though under imperfect or monopolistic competition each firm has its own clientele, one of the important consequences of this regular supplier/clientele relationship is that the firm must avoid, at all costs, giving the impression of over-charging, i.e., of its clients having made a bad bargain by

---

*The figures have also shown that there were a small proportion of firms (1 percent of the total) who had losses.

sticking to the firm. Hence, price-wise they must be competitive to retain the need for their regular relationship—but on account of good personal relationships with their customers, not of the impersonal relationships of Walrasian markets.

Just what are the reasons for these differences in the share of profits between different firms? One school of thought (of which the German economist, Hanns Joachim Rüstow, is the most prominent adherent) attributes it to embodied technical progress combined with the fact that in each period only a small part of the extant capital equipment is renewed, so that the production in any one period is manufactured by a combination of numerous older and newer technologies. However, to account for a difference of as much as 4:1, the oldest equipment still in use must be very old indeed: with an annual growth of labor productivity of say 3 percent, it requires a period of 47 years for productivity to become four times as high. A more important reason is that if the differences in profitability were only the consequence of the use of modern versus obsolete equipment, it would surely pay firms to spread their investment over time in such a way that the average age of their equipment reflects the average in the industry, so that it would operate with average costs, earning average profit. Another school of thought, represented by Professor Leibenstein, attributes the differences to managerial efficiency. It is difficult to believe, however, that managerial efficiency can be the cause of differences in costs of such order, since inefficient managers would lose their jobs sooner or later. Finally, the differences may simply represent differences in capacity utilization due to differences in accidental factors, such as the selling appeal of some particular design, the quality of advertising, or just bad luck.

Okun's Law

Whatever the cause, the important question is how to reconcile these figures with Okun's famous Law. In its original form it stated that a 1 percent reduction in the unemployment rate will be associated with a 3.2 percent increase in real G.N.P., which, after making due allowance for the relationship of changes in employment to weekly man-hours worked and to changes in unemployment, amounts to saying that a 1 percent increase in employment (measured in man-hours) is associated with a 2 percent increase in output; this comes very close to the relationship that has become known as the Verdoorn Law. However, Okun's Law was derived from time series data, and his own interpretation of it was that the short-period productivity gain associated with an increase in output is largely a reflection of the economies gained from higher capacity utilization, mainly on account of the importance of "overhead labor" in total labor costs. The Verdoorn Law on the other hand compares the productivity growth differences associated with different trend-rates of growth as between different regions or countries, the periods being so chosen that the cyclical element in the productivity change should be eliminated as far as possible, for example, by taking the period between successive peak years in the cycle when the degree of capacity utilization was approximately the same in the initial and final years.

However, from our present point of view, what is important is the short-term productivity change associated with changes in demand, and how two kinds of evidence can be reconciled with one another. One kind is that which relates to a hierarchy of establishments and firms, in ascending order of costs (or descending order of productivity), which would suggest, in conformity with the basic tenets of neoclassical theory, that short-term marginal costs are increasing (or that marginal productivity is diminishing, which comes to the same thing). The other is the relationship represented by Okun's Law, which suggests that in the short-term, output and productivity are positively correlated, not negatively.

If we allow for imperfect competition it is possible, if all firms have the *same* cost curves, for average costs to fall with increasing output, so that average productivity will rise with increasing output. (Marginal productivity is not relevant in this case, since as long as average productivity is rising, marginal productivity can have no role in the firm's decision making.)* The case of imperfect competition with a hierarchy of firms of varying cost levels and efficiency has, as far as I know, never been generally considered but one would expect, in a manner analogous to the perfect competition case, that the least efficient firms bear the brunt of a reduction of output, in which case again the Okun relationship should indicate a coefficient that is less than unity and not greater than unity.

However, the stylized facts derived from observa-

---

*The marginal revenue product, a notion often mentioned by Okun, has no relevance to this situation, since it registers the extra revenue obtained by the single firm from a small increase in output when *all other firm's* outputs are assumed to be constant; it has no relevance to the case when there is an increase in demand, affecting all firms equally.

tions suggest that when there is a recession or a slump, *all* firms suffer a loss of demand, and the reduction of output is distributed among the different firms more or less equally, and not concentrated on the inefficient tail of the industry. (There are exceptions to this under a severe contraction such as Britain has experienced under Mrs. Thatcher, when a proportion of establishments is closed down altogether; this is bound to improve the average.)

The explanation for this apparently irrational result is simple. The relatively inefficient firms suffer the penalty of low profits, which means that from the point of view of the *buyer* it is a matter of indifference whether he buys from a high-cost or a low-cost firm. The high-cost firm can compete effectively with the low-cost firm because its inefficiency is not reflected in its prices, only in its profits. Hence, when demand expands, productivity rises because the rise in output following the rise in demand is shared among *all* firms, not concentrated among the marginal firms.

You may say that this is not a *rational* arrangement; in any rational scheme production should be concentrated in the most efficient units, and hence any expansion should mean resorting to the less efficient. This is what Keynes assumed in the *General Theory*, and, when he was finally persuaded that this assumption did not hold, he exclaimed in despair that he "always regarded decreasing physical returns in the short period as one of the incontrovertible propositions of our miserable subject!"*

*Notes on Ohlin, John Maynard Keynes, *Collected Writings*, Vol. 14, p. 190.

How Competition Works

In probing this situation further we are treading on difficult ground and anything one can say (or at least *I* can say) is rather tentative. Nobody really knows the answers to the most important questions—they are important because they go to the heart of the matter of how competition works in a modern industrial economy. I think I can best tackle the field by making a number of points.

(1) There can be no doubt that firms operate in imperfect markets where customer relationships are very important. Here I very much agree with Okun's view: a firm will make a great effort to build up a regular clientele, and having built it up, to keep it by giving value for money, whether in the quality or reliability of the product, or its price relative to the products of other firms, taking its reputation for quality, reliability, etc. into account. This means that while each firm decides on its own selling prices, its freedom of choice is very much restricted by other firms. It must choose the "right price" from its own point of view, and this of course is greatly dependent on what is being offered by others.

(2) Given this fact, it is a simplification to say that prices are *cost-determined*. They are cost-determined in the sense that all firms raise their prices more or less in the same proportion when costs—wages or material costs—go up, but they are not cost-determined in the sense that the price of each firm is arrived at by adding a markup to direct costs or total costs, a markup that is both constant and rigid—constant between firms and rigid over time. Any firm that knows there is a "right price" to choose—given the choices offered in the

market—does not really follow markup pricing. The markup is in fact a residual between its own costs and the price chosen on market considerations. On this point I feel compelled to disagree with Okun's emphatic conclusion that "markup rigidity is too pervasive across the U.S. economy to be attributable to oligopoly" or that the kinked demand curve, which can provide an explanation for rigid prices, is a "feature of clientele relationship rather than oligopoly."* Barring the case when the direct costs per unit of different firms are the same at standard volumes (and I mention this as a possibility that cannot be ruled out if the main reason for differences in profit shares are differences in *sales in relation to capacity*, and not differences in costs at the *same* capacity utilization) the kinked demand curve *cannot* explain where the price is in relation to costs, precisely because the kink is where the price is—if the price were somewhere else, so would be the kink in the demand curve. (Given the price, the kinked demand curve can explain why a change in demand, up or down, leaves the price unchanged, which is a different matter.) But to explain the price, and therefore the *position* of the kink, one must suppose that there is some firm, or possibly a *group* of firms, that exercise a position of price leadership; it is these firms that are free to decide on their markup over costs, and thereby set a standard for prices that other firms must follow.

(3) When I mentioned a "group of firms" I had Marshall's concept of a "representative firm" in mind. This concept assumes that in each industry a large part of the output is produced by firms of *average* managerial

*Ibid., p. 176.

efficiency, using equipment of *average* age, and workers of *average* ability. In other words, while the difference between the most efficient and the least efficient firms is very large, neither of them are decisive for the determination of prices; these are determined by the behavior of the "representative firm" which sets the standard for all the others, and, whether acting in tacit collusion or quite independently, makes the level and structure of prices in the industry what it is.

But how do they arrive at the markup? It is vain to look for this in the traditional view that there is a particular price that maximizes their profits, given by the well-known formula $e/e-1$, where e stands for the point-elasticity of their (unkinked) demand curves. In the first place, they have no demand curve, not only because they are ignorant (which is also true) but because the demand curve for the products of the firm presupposes that all *other* firms' prices were given or else they are all identical with the price-making firm's price and neither of these assumptions can be taken for granted. A more important reason is that maximizing the present value of their future prospects means, in a growing economy, maximizing the attainable *rate of growth of their profits*, which may require a different markup from maximizing their current profit.

Maximizing the Growth Rate of Profits

This objective—maximizing the attainable rate of growth—can mean several things. First, it means aiming at a price that will maintain, and, if possible, improve on their *share* of the market. This consideration would suggest that they should choose a price and hence a markup that is as *low* as they can make it.

Second, they must choose a markup that allows them to increase their *own* capital, by means of ploughed-back profits as much as possible, subject to the safeguard of being able to have recourse to external equity finance if, despite their efforts, the increase in their own capital proves insufficient to keep in step with the increase in their market. This second consideration taken by itself suggests making the markup as high as possible, since the higher the markup, the higher the rate at which their own capital accumulates at any given plough-back ratio. The plough-back ratio, on this view—and this is perhaps the least firmly established part of the theory—depends on their view of the importance of maintaining a "safeguard" of access to external finance if that proves necessary. For that reason they aim at a *constant* plough-back ratio, which means raising dividends in line with earnings.* Their main motive in all this is to prevent a situation from arising whereby they become restricted in their expansion by a financial constraint—by having to borrow too much, or having to raise equity capital on terms that make them an attractive target for take-over bids.

I realize that in existing literature this particular consideration for determining the price-leader's markup—the need to build up capital from internal sources—is hardly ever considered, simply because internal and external sources of equity finance are considered as near-perfect substitutes for one another. This may be true in the dreamworld of perfect knowledge, perfect foresight, and no risk or uncertainty. Unfortunately, in the real world such perfections are absent and it is

---

*Another stylized fact: while firms differ widely in their payout ratio, most firms tend to maintain it at a constant rate, i.e., to increase their dividends in line with earnings.

more correct to regard the sources of internal and external finance as being in a complementary relationship, and not as substitutes.

So these opposing considerations should determine the firm's judgment as to what the optimum markup should be. Perhaps I ought to add a third consideration which might also weigh in the balance: the ability to wage a price-war, the possibility of which can never be excluded. These are likely to arise as a result of the appearance of new products introduced by newcomers, which may have to be resisted by considerable price-cutting. This ability varies in inverse proportion to the share of direct costs to the selling price, since the price can be reduced only up to the point where it cuts into the currently incurred costs of labor and materials. The scope for material savings may not be large, but labor costs can be reduced by the use of more capital-intensive techniques which may involve a higher capital expenditure per unit of output. (This, as I shall argue in the next lecture, is not usually the case under increasing returns.) The maintenance of any given rate of capacity expansion will require a higher rate of growth in (financial) reserves; this consideration would thus also argue for a relatively high markup.

All this is largely speculative. We *do* know that in the very great majority of cases the producers or sellers are price-makers and quantity-takers; we *do* know that this fact in itself shows that markets are imperfect; but we do not know how far different sellers compete on a price basis, whether there is price-leadership, or whether the relative rigidity of prices in the face of large variations in selling volume is mainly motivated by defensive considerations, the promotion of good relations with their customers, or some other factor of this kind. And we have no sufficient explanation for the fact that prices maintain a fairly constant relationship to costs, cost increases due to higher wages or material prices being passed on very promptly. Changes in selling volumes, on the other hand, are only likely to cause price changes when they are the result of the appearance of new sources of competition, not when they are part of a general change in demand.

Conformity of Pattern

Finally, we do not really know the causes of the uniformity in pattern which emerged in the last 50 years, under which not more than three large firms account for the great majority of total sales (perhaps 70 to 80 percent of the total or more) while the remainder is divided among a large number of small firms (normally, several hundreds). This pattern emerged in so many different industries—like manufacturers of automobiles and other durable consumer goods such as vacuum cleaners, refrigerators, electric light bulbs, or even newspapers or advertising agencies—that there must be some explanation in the dynamics of competition that goes beyond the considerations usually taken into account. Clearly, increasing returns to scale has in a broad sense something to do with it, but that cannot be the whole explanation, since the numbers seem to be similar in countries as different as the United States or Switzerland. One may find (I am putting this as a hypothesis) that the leading producers have the same market share in both countries, even though the size of the market is 20 to 30 times as large in one case as in the other.

I am sure that empirical research of the right kind

will, in time, considerably improve our knowledge of how modern market economies work. But it will require new methods of research that would make greater use of knowledge gained through personal contact and on-the-job investigations, and less on the testing of formal models through statistics and econometrics. There is an enormous amount of empirical research going on but it is stifled by operating *within* the framework of established theory.

III

Interregional Trade
and
Cumulative Causation

I will begin the last lecture with an attempt to explain (and justify) the title of these lectures which was meant to imply that the prevailing methods of analyzing how a market economy functions have led to a "cul-de-sac." Far from improving our understanding with the gradual accumulation of empirical knowledge and experience, this blind alley has actually inhibited the progress of useful knowledge; it has created a serious brake on the development of economic thought.

By the term "useful" I do not just mean that it did not help the "decision makers," whether in the public or the private field, in arriving at the right decisions. Though the ultimate justification of scientific inquiry, whether in the natural or the social field, is to improve our power over the enviroment, additions to knowledge are useful even if they do not have any immediate application, so long as they enable one to construct improved "models" that highlight the critical aspects of how things work.

In the field of economics, the post-World War II period was a remarkable contrast to the great innovative period of the 1930s. There was a tremendous growth of mathematical economics, based on highly sophisticated techniques, such as the use of fixed-point theorems, minmax solutions, game theoretical techniques, etc., a great deal of which originated in the papers of one of the great mathematicians of the century, John von Neumann.

Marshall's View on the Use of Mathematics in Economics

Was this a healthy or promising development? It is at this stage that I should like to quote the views of Alfred Marshall on the use of mathematics in economics, which were not taken much notice of for quite some time, not until the publication of Guillebaud's *variorum* edition of the *Principles*, and his associated correspondence with other economists brought a revival of interest in Marshall's views on how economics should be pursued. Marshall was a brilliant mathematician, he was Second Wrangler in the Mathematical Tripos in the same year Lord Rayleigh was First Wrangler, and he taught mathematics as a Fellow of St. John's College before he took up economics. His *magnum opus*, the *Principles* on which he worked for ten years, appeared in 1890. In 1906, or 16 years later, after the *Principles* went through five separate editions, he wrote in a letter to A. L. Bowley:

> I had a growing feeling in the later years of my work that a good mathematical theorem dealing with economic hypotheses was very unlikely to be good economics, and I went more and more on the rules—(1) Use mathematics as a shorthand language, rather than as an engine of inquiry. (2) Keep these till you

have done. (3) Translate into English. (4) Then illustrate by examples that are important in real life. (5) Burn the mathematics. (6) If you can't succeed in (4), burn (3). This last I did often.*

He also wrote:

In my view every economic fact, whether or not it is of such a nature as to be expressed in numbers, stands in relation as cause and effect to many other facts; and since it never happens that all of them can be expressed in numbers, the application of exact mathematical methods to those that can is nearly always a waste of time, while in the large majority of cases it is particularly misleading; and the world would have been further on its way forward if the work had never been done at all.**

The world—and economics as a subject—has changed a great deal since these words were written. Yet Marshall's *Principles* seem to me an infinitely more valuable work than Walras's *Elements* or Pareto's *Manual*, even though it may not be equal to these two as a source of inspiration to later generations. Marshall realized that human societies are subject to continuous evolution, the precise direction of which can never be predicted; and he frequently emphasized that economics has far more in common with biology than with mechanics: "the laws of biology, like those of economics, vary much in definiteness, in range of application and in certainty."† He also said that "law" in social science is no more than a "statement of social tendencies."

*Guillebaud, *Marshall's Principles of Economics*, Vol. 2 (Notes), p. 775.
**Ibid, p. 774.
†*Principles*, 4th ed., p. 104.

A Mathematical Crystal

However, as I already explained in the first lecture, post-World War II developments in economics were in sharp contrast to Marshall's method of keeping theoretical work in close contact with reality, even at the cost of sacrificing the strict logical consistency of its main propositions. In sharp contrast to this method, the postwar development of the theory of competitive equilibrium consisted mainly in setting up a logically watertight system, with its precise number of necessary axioms that formed, to use Heisenberg's words, "a mathematical crystal" which cannot be further improved or perfected—"some rigid thing, which may be correct or incorrect but without an intermediate case." General equilibrium theory achieved this state of becoming a "mathematical crystal" by 1954. Since then nothing important has been added to it (unless it is the rational expectations hypothesis, though I doubt this could really be incorporated in the formal theory as an additional axiom), but nothing has come of the original intention to gradually "dismantle the scaffolding" and to show the main conclusions in a form that can be verified by econometric methods, and after allowing for those features of reality—such as imperfect competition and increasing returns to scale—which have been excluded by the original set of axioms. On the contrary, it was demonstrated that neither increasing returns to scale nor imperfect competition could be accommodated within the Walrasian framework. It would be truer to say that the fascination exerted by the neo-Walrasian system on the academic community created the opposite kind of movement: the economic theorists' view of reality became increasingly distorted, so as to come closer to the theoretical image rather than the other way round. If Mahomet cannot go to the mountain then the mountain must be brought to Mahomet. So neoclassical theorists increasingly claim to believe that competition is virtually, if not actually, perfect; that production functions are linear and that markets *are* continuously market-clearing, and everyone behaves as if one has the right answer to every question, except for stochastic misperceptions.

The Nature of Time

It seems clear that if we are to get out of the present *impasse* we must begin by constructing a different kind of abstract model, one that recognizes from the beginning that time is a continuing and irreversible process; that it is impossible to assume the constancy of anything *over* time, such as the supply of labor or capital, the psychological preferences for commodities, the nature and number of commodities, or technical knowledge. All these things are in a continuous process of change but the forces that make for change are endogenous not exogenous to the system. The only truly exogenous factor is *whatever exists at a given moment of time,* as a heritage of the past. This includes all material things, whether the products of nature, or man, or a combination of them, i.e., all forms of capital, as embodied in building, factories, or machines; the available supply of labor—workers, managers, scientists, with all kinds of qualifications and skill. All these in existence at the present moment, the heritage of all past history, determine what can be produced or created in the immediate future, say in the next day, and that, together with what exists now, determines the range of alternatives for the day after, and so on. Taking the very near future, anything that can be produced is determined, or rather limited, by the heritage of the past: the stocks of flour at the hands of the bakers today will determine the bread that can be produced tomorrow. The heritage of the past is the one truly exogenous factor, and its influence will determine future events to an extent that varies *inversely* with the distance of the future period from the present. Thus our ability to predict what *can* happen or what is likely to happen becomes progressively less as we consider the more distant future as against the nearer future.

The very notion of equilibrium, particularly of long-run equilibrium, amounts to a *denial* of this—for this notion asserts that the operation of economic forces is constrained by a set of exogenous variables which are given from the outside, so to speak, and which remain stable over time. In other words, equilibrium theory assumes that the environment in which economic forces operate is imposed on the system from outside, and it is something different from a historical heritage; indeed, as is often emphasized, the exogenous variables that determine the nature of equilibrium are independent of history in their most important characteristics. Any given constellation of such exogenous variables, whatever the initial situation, will inevitably lead, perhaps through a succession of steps (succession of "temporary equilibria"), to a *unique point* of final equilibrium, the exact nature of which, both as regards the price system and output system, can be deduced from the "data," the set of exogenous variables, the operation of which is confined by strictly formulated axioms. Continuous growth can only be thought of within this intellectual framework as a steady state, where everything grows in exact proportion, though what the proportions are, or what the growth rate is, is itself the outcome of economic forces, as in von Neumann's celebrated growth model.

However, the two really important things Neumann's model was *not* capable of dealing with is continuous change in knowledge and the existence of non-linearities in productive activities, in other words, increasing returns.

Increasing Returns

These two phenomena are to a considerable extent involved in one another. In economics everything is, as Marshall emphasized, both cause and effect. The progress of knowledge, which appears as the spontaneous product of the human brain, is very often the result gained from experience—learning by doing. And as the great American economist, Allyn Young, emphasized in his famous paper *Increasing Returns and Economic Progress*, published shortly before his early death in the winter of 1928-29—a paper which for reasons that are not clear to me did not have the influence in his native country that it so clearly deserved*—once we allow for increasing returns, the laws of economics take on quite a different appearance. Whereas previously change—whether a change in tastes or in technical knowledge—was generally ascribed to some exogenous factor, and analyzed by the well-known technique of comparative statics, given the existence of increasing

*The paper was read as the Presidential address to Section F of the British Association in Glasgow, in September 1928, and published in the December 1928 issue of the *Economic Journal*.

returns, the forces making for continued change and development are endogenous:

> They are engendered from within the economic system. No analysis of the forces making for economic equilibrium, forces that we might say are tangential at any moment of time, will serve to illumine this field, for movements away from equilibrium, departures from previous trends are characteristic of it.

Young regarded Adam Smith's famous theorem (the title to the third chapter of Book I of the *Wealth of Nations*) that the "division of labour is limited by the extent of the market" as "one of the most illuminating and fruitful generalisations which can be found anywhere in the whole literature of economics." In fact, he takes it as his text, "in much the same way that some minor composer borrows a theme from one of the masters and adds certain developments or variations of his own." No one, as far as he knew, tried to enumerate all the different aspects of the division of labor, and he himself was mainly concerned with two aspects: the growth of indirect or roundabout methods of production and the division of labor among industries.

He thought that Smith missed the main point in emphasizing the improvement in techniques that occur to workmen engaged in specialized routine operations. He said, "The important thing of course is that with the division of labour a group of complex processes is transformed into a succession of simple processes, some of which, at least, lend themselves to the use of machinery." In the use of machinery and the adoption of indirect processes, there is a further division of labor, the economies of which are again limited by the extent of the market. Quoting Young:

It would be wasteful to make a hammer to drive a single nail; it would be better to use whatever awkward implement lies conveniently at hand. It would be wasteful to furnish a factory with elaborate equipment of specially constructed jigs, gauges, lathes, drills, presses and conveyors to build a hundred automobiles; it would be better to rely mostly upon tools and machines of standard types so as to make relatively larger use of directly-applied and a relatively smaller use of indirectly-applied labour. Mr. Ford's methods would be absurdly uneconomical if his output were very small and would be unprofitable even if his output were what many other manufacturers of automobiles would call large.

Here Young enunciates a very important proposition, the significance of which is not appreciated even today. "Roundabout" methods of production imply the use of more capital in relation to labor. This was emphasized first by the Austrians and was the basis of Böhm-Bawerk's capital theory. But what Böhm and the Austrians have not seen is that the capital/labor ratio is not a matter of deriving the "optimal point" on some production function depending on the relative scarcities and hence the relative prices of the two factors (wages and the interest rate). It is a matter of using the cheapest method of production given the *size of the market*. It is the size of the market, and not the given (aggregate) endowment of capital relative to labor that determines how much capital will be used in relation to labor.

The Size of the Market

The size of the market is not a datum, it is *not* exogenous to the individual producers who operate the system. Young said:

It is dangerous to assign to any single factor the leading role in that continuing economic revolution which has taken the modern world so far away from the world of a few hundred years ago. But is there any other factor which has a better claim to that role than the persistent search for markets? No other hypothesis so well unites economic history and economic theory. It is sometimes said that while in the Middle Ages and in the early modern period industry was the servant of commerce, since the rise of "industrial capitalism" the relation has been reversed, commerce being now merely an agent of industry. If this means that finding markets is one of the tasks of modern industry, it is true. If it means that industry imposes its will upon the market, that whereas formerly the things which were produced were the things which would be sold, now the things which have to be sold are the things that are produced, it is not true.

(All I would add here is that in the following half-century this conclusion became less clear-cut than it appeared to Young in the 1920s.)

No doubt when Ford invented and marketed the Model T Ford America was a country with a large number of farmers to whom the possession of an automobile, if they could afford it, was very convenient. The great achievement of Ford was to design an automobile that farmers could afford to buy. He did so by designing techniques of production that enormously increased the ratio of capital to labor: the amount of capital used per worker was very much greater than with the then prevailing techniques of making motorcars. But while the capital/labor ratio increased enormously, the capital/output ratio did not, as it necessarily would have done if the increase in labor productivity was a matter of substituting capital for labor along a neoclassical production function. Instead, Young's contention that the amount of capital per worker is a matter of the division of labor, and that in turn depends on, and reflects, the size of the market, is (in my view) brilliantly supported by one of the best established "stylized facts" of capitalist development: that while the capital/labor ratio is rising more or less in proportion to productivity, and it is highest among the richest nations and lowest among the poorest, the capital/output ratio is much the same as between poor and rich countries—it is no higher in America (on some estimates it is lower) than it is in India.

Capital and Output Grow Together

The simple point is that with an increase in the division of labor, capital and output grow together. The capital/labor ratio is a by-product of high productivity resulting from large production; it has nothing to do with marginal productivities or marginal rates of substitution, concepts that only make sense under the wholly artificial assumption of constant returns to scale.

Of course the success of the Model T Ford meant a tremendous accumulation of capital, which would not have taken place otherwise. Of course this accumulation required a lot of savings, and the savings were the profits of the Ford Motor Co. which (in the critical years of expansion) were ploughed back into the business to the extent of 90 or 95 percent. But the savings, the accumulation, the adoption of highly capital intensive techniques were all consequences of a successful search for markets which enabled Ford to exploit the economies of large-scale production.

> Although the initial displacement may be considerable and the repercussions upon particular industries unfavorable [think of the horse and buggy industry], the enlarging of the market for any one commodity produced under conditions of increasing returns generally has the net effect, as I have tried to show, of enlarging the market for other commodities. The businessman's mercantilistic emphasis upon markets may have a sounder basis than the economist, who thinks mostly in terms of economic statics, is prone to admit. How far "selling expenses," for example, are to be counted sheer economic waste depends on their effect on the aggregate product of industry, as distinguished from their effects upon the fortunes of particular undertakings.

The existence of increasing returns, even if confined to particular sectors of an economy, such as manufacturing, are bound to cause very large differences to the reaction pattern of the economy. There is no inherent tendency to anything that could be called an equilibrium, or an equilibrium path. The state of the economy at any one point of time cannot be "predicted" except as a result of the sequence of events that led up to it; the successive chains in that sequence might not have occurred but for the new opportunities created by previous developments.

As Young emphasized, the influences responsible for increasing returns are continually reinforced by the discovery of new natural resources and the uses for them, and the growth of scientific knowledge in general. "The causal connection between the growth of industry and the progress of science runs in both directions, but on which side the preponderant influence lies no one can say." Moreover the process is accompanied by a continual subdivision of industries and the growth of specialist firms at intermediate stages of production who come to serve the needs of several different industries simultaneously. Hence:

> Over a large part of the field of industry an increasingly intricate nexus of specialised undertakings has inserted itself between the producer of the raw material and the consumer of the final product. With the extension of the division of labour among industries, the representative firm, like the industry of which it is a part, loses its identity. Its internal economies dissolve into the internal and external economies of the more highly specialised undertakings which are its successors and are supplemented by new economies.

The points that Young did not emphasize but that are very important (in my view) are first, that this process tends to cluster around geographic centers (which may be thought of as cities, and in a wider sense, countries as political entities); this is presumably so because its success largely depends on the presence of specialized manpower, and the stimulus derived from continuous and easy communication between men with similar experience, as well as joint production between small specialized firms which involves frequent transfer of an unfinished product between numerous specialized firms.* Second, this

*George Stigler, *Journal of Political Economy*, 1951, pp. 192–193, quoting G. C. Allen on the *Industrial Development of Birmingham 1860-1927*; also the quotation from Benjamin Franklin on p. 193. fn.

kind of "dynamic" economies of scale do not extend to all forms of economic activity but are largely concentrated on manufacturing industry. They have no equivalent in agriculture, even though technical progress in agriculture is equally the joint result of experience and the progress of scientific knowledge, but their realization does not depend, or only to a minor extent, on the size of the market; and they do not really extend to services—at least the part of "services" connected with the transport and distribution of goods—even though their methods of production are equally subject to continual change, as the spread of supermarkets, self-service stores, cafeterias, and so on, testifies. However, there can be no doubt that manufacturing is the true engine of growth; the greater spread of scientific and technical knowledge, which is both a consequence and a cause of continued progress in manufacturing, reinforces this tendency to "polarization" of industrial activities.*

At the same time, since success in industrial development is unlikely to be the same as between different industries in the same "center," or as between the same industry in different "centers," the very process of development occurring at different places gives scope for mutually advantageous exchanges between different areas (or countries, if you like), with each area exporting those products where its comparative advantage is the highest. This statement is similar in formulation, but as we shall see presently, by no means identical, to the classical theory of comparative costs,

---

*Major scientific discoveries (like Faraday's invention of the electric dynamo) are clearly causes of subsequent industrial development. But innumerable minor discoveries *result* from industrial activities, as well as being the cause of changes in activities.

or its modern equivalent, including Samuelson's "factor price equalization theorem." With the reduction of the cost of transportation and the easing of other barriers to trade, such as tariffs, the scope for international trade in "substitutes" (goods that *could* be produced in the importing country as well as the exporting country) has become enormously enlarged. The increase in international trade of manufactures in the post-World War II period has been much greater as between manufacturing countries—in intermediate products for industrial goods as well as in finished goods—than between manufacturing countries and primary producers. So long as such trade is balanced—with each country exporting as much as it is importing—it is bound to operate so as to enhance the division of labor and accelerate the growth of the total market. There are a number of factors, however, that create spontaneous tendencies to imbalance which may well mean that the growth of some of the participants is enhanced while the growth of others is diminished. In contrast to the classical theory of international trade, free trade or even a reduction of barriers to trade may stunt the growth of some industrial areas and enhance the growth of others. Free trade therefore is not necessarily to the benefit of each participant, as it is under the theories of Ricardo, John Stuart Mill, Hekscher, Ohlin, or Samuelson. If we look at the postwar world, there were a number of countries, of which Japan is most conspicuous, who dramatically increased their share of world trade, and there were others, including both the United States and the United Kingdom, but particularly the latter, whose industrial expansion was diminished in consequence.

This could not happen of course under classical

assumptions, where trade is bound to benefit all participants—even though, as Mill showed, the benefit need not be equally shared; it could be much greater for some participants than for others. But under the innocent-sounding assumption of constant returns to scale, equal technical knowledge to all parties (that is, identity of production functions) comparative cost differences could only arise as a result of differences in the relative scarcities, and hence the relative prices, of the different factors of production. International trade is bound to reduce these differences (since each country will export those goods requiring more of the factors of production that are relatively more abundant) and import goods with the opposite characteristics. As a result, the differences in factor price ratios are bound to be reduced, and in favorable circumstances (such as completely free trade, no transport costs) will be eliminated altogether. On these conditions free trade in goods is a complete substitute to completely free mobility factors, and *vice versa*.

Differences in Productivities
May Be Enlarged by Trade

Alas, in the world of increasing returns this is not so. In this latter case it is not the differences in the relative prices of factors that are important, but relative differences in labor productivities (measured in terms of a common currency) which, even in the absence of any differences in capital productivities (in the amount of capital employed per unit of output) will make the country with the higher productivity a favorable one for exports and a relatively unfavorable one for imports. It will therefore tend to have a surplus of exports over imports. In the other industrial centers with which it trades, the opposite will take place. This in itself will serve to generate forces tending to eliminate such differences, even in the absence of any political action aimed at securing a balance in the international flow of payments.

So far we have said nothing about the territorial (or regional) aspects of economic development. In a pure Walrasian model the spatial distribution of economic activities is not considered as such though I suppose that space, in the shape of "land," lurks in the background, since many of the "products" are of a nature in which land or natural resources (in the form of minerals) play a prominent part in their production; and formally, products available at different points of space are considered to be different products. In theoretical models (other than those explicitly devoted to problems of international trade) it is generally assumed (as it is in Keynes) that the "economy" one is considering is a "closed economy" so as to exclude problems connected with exports and imports. However, if we imagine a closed economy containing several industrial centers, as well as a land area that supplies agricultural and mineral products to these industrial centers, much the same problems arise, with the difference only that we assume a single currency,i.e., that all prices are expressed in the same *numeraire*.

If imbalances arise in trade, because one industrial center's exports are larger than its imports, whereas with the other centers imports exceed exports, the export surplus area will tend to expand production because realized receipts will exceed planned receipts causing producers to expand; this will cause imports to rise (since the use of imported commodities will expand in line with the others), causing the export surplus to diminish, and hence the excess of realized over planned receipts to diminish, until a balance is reached, with exports equaling imports. In the other countries, the reverse process takes place: output and incomes will be reduced in successive steps until imports are reduced to the level of exports.

The same story could be told in dynamic terms in which the growth rate is accelerated in response to an excess of export growth over import growth, and this acceleration will go on with gradually diminishing speed until the growth rate rises enough for the growth of imports to become equal to the growth of exports. With the other countries, the same process takes place in reverse. Thus growth rates are decelerated until the growth of imports is reduced to the same rate as the growth of exports.

However, under the general assumption of increasing returns, this is not the end of the story. If we started with the arbitrary assumption that the various industrial centers expanded at the same rate, we now have a situation in which one of the centers at least grows at a faster rate than the others. Hence its productivity growth will be accelerated and unless its domestic absorption (meaning its domestic consumption and investment) keeps pace with its faster productivity growth, its export surplus will reappear, giving rise to another push, making for faster growth rates for itself and slower growth rates for the others.

Cumulative Causation

This, in the briefest outline, is the principle of cumulative causation whereby some regions gain at the expense of others, leading to increasing inequalities between relatively prosperous and relatively poor areas. It has no place in Walrasian economics simply because it has no place under the general assumption of constant returns to scale.

When Allyn Young wrote his paper it was a year before the Wall Street Crash (which he didn't live to see), and no doubt his views were greatly influenced by the fact that he lived through the period of the fastest growth in the American economy; at a time when the role of the government in guiding the economy (through fiscal or monetary measures) was at its minimum; when with rapid growth went rapid population growth through immigration and equally rapid capital accumulation, largely financed (except for public utilities, railways and so on) out of the profits of enterprise. The question of whether the "economic progress" resulting from the joint influence of scientific progress and industrial growth was as high as it could be or whether it could be further improved by well formulated and judiciously chosen public policies is not one that occurred to Young. Nor did he deal with the problem of cyclical fluctuations, which was a prominent feature of the American scene, even during its most hectic periods of economic growth. He did mention that the very size of America as measured not by area nor by the number of inhabitants but by the size of its aggregate product, makes it easier to develop the division of labor as compared with say, England, whose possibilities were more constrained.

Arthur Okun lived in a different world. Up to the First World War America did not really experience unemployment on a serious scale, except in periods of cyclical recession, and these were relatively short. The fluctuations in the aggregate demand for labor (which were considerable) were mainly reflected in variations of the immigration figures, which meant that they affected the fortunes of the prospective immigrant far more than the indigenous working population.* Despite industrialization, America produced a growing surplus of grains, leading to a large and growing purchasing power of the farming population, which provided the source of a growing demand for manufactured goods. The exchange of manufactures with primary products produced in the colonies, which was such an important feature of the British economy, took place *within* America, in the growing demand for food by the urban areas, and the growing demand for manufactures by the rural areas.

The Great Depression changed all that, and for reasons that are not clear even now, America led the world into a state of recession which produced 15 million unemployed in America, 3½ million in Britain, and 7 million in Germany. It led to Hitler's rise to power in Germany and thus, indirectly, to the Second World War. And the fact that the gross national product in real terms nearly doubled in the United States in the three years between the last prewar year and the first postwar year shows that the conventional measures underestimated the extent to which actual output fell short of potential output.

In the postwar period, partly under the influence of Keynesian economics, but mainly on account of the fear

*The American example of the supply of labor responding to the demand for labor through immigration, though more dramatic, was qualitatively no different from the growth of all successful industrial centers, the manufacturing industries of which attracted labor both from the countryside (agriculture) and from disguised unemployment in services.

of a return to the prewar situation of economic stagnation and mass unemployment, it was generally accepted (in some countries more explicitly than in others) that the government should use the fiscal weapon and the monetary weapon through variation of interest rates so as to maintain the growth of effective demand necessary to secure continual full employment (or reasonably full employment) together with a steady rise in the standards of well-being, achieved through the growth of output and productivity. The question was not whether it is possible to secure these objectives— for the first two postwar decades it was generally believed that it was—but how to achieve them consistently with the minimum of economic inequality necessary to provide the incentives that make a capitalist system (or a socialist system, for that matter) work. Okun's 1970 book *The Political Economy of Prosperity*, for all its criticism of the nature or timing of past policies, and for the gap between realized output and the output that could have been attained by more apropriate and better timed policy measures, was animated by a strong underlying optimism in the possibility of maintaining prosperity and monetary stability at the same time—by selecting a compromise target that allows some unemployment—at 4 percent or so—that would be sufficient to secure the gradual liquidation of inflation over a period of years.

In the final chapter of his posthumously published book, drafted ten years later, this optimism is far more circumscribed. Okun recognizes that combating inflation and unemployment needs instruments or institutions that go beyond the use of fiscal and monetary policies as economic stabilizers, and he pins his hopes on measures that act directly on prices and wages.

Unfortunately these final suggestions are not as well developed as they no doubt would have been if his thinking on these matters had not been cut short by his sudden death. He was clearly feeling his way to measures acting on prices through international buffer stock schemes (in the case of grains and possibly other commodities) and to the avoidance of cost-raising indirect taxation (like financing social insurance other than through payroll taxes on the employer), possibly supplemented by subsidies or negative indirect taxes and tax-based incomes policies, though none of these suggestions received strong endorsement.

Inflationary Expectations

My own feeling is that the major new element of the 1970s was inflationary expectations, and the volatility of expectations, not those relating to consumer prices and the cost of living but to the prices of staple products, raw materials, and energy, which directly or indirectly enter into costs. As I mentioned already in my first lecture, after 1971 raw material prices rose sharply at the first sign of increased demand and fell steeply at the first signs of a recession; the sensitivity of prices to changes in world industrial production was three times as high as before. This instability may have had something to do with the suspension of the gold standard; so long as the dollar remained convertible to gold (even if only in a very restricted form) the commodity dealers' belief in the existence of a long-run normal price for commodities was not destroyed; inflationary trends, even if prolonged, were more likely to be treated as temporary affairs. (The average level of commodity prices moving in international trade, as measured by the U. N. index, was much the *same* in dollar terms in 1970 as in 1950. It was only in 1971/72 that an explosive rise of commodity prices began; this preceded the "oil-shock" at the end of 1973.) Now that no currency is convertible except into other currencies and then at constantly varying exchange rates, there is no form of money that can be expected to remain stable in terms of real value. In these circumstances only international measures aiming at stabilizing the prices of commodities by means of buffer stocks schemes, linked to an international reserve currency such as the SDR, offer (in my view) any hope of a radical improvement.

The other great cause of inflation, the excessive increase rate of money wages relative to productivity increases, could be tackled, I believe, by tying the workers' material interests more directly to the success of the enterprise that employs them; for example, giving an appreciable part of the wage-earners' remuneration in the form of a bonus—a common system in Japan—that is geared to the company's profits measured, if possible, in constant prices.

I throw out these suggestions in the hope of stimulating discussion, particularly on how Arthur Okun would have reacted to these ideas in view of the world economic stagnation of the last few years.